DATE DUE

NATURE DETECTIVE
Weather

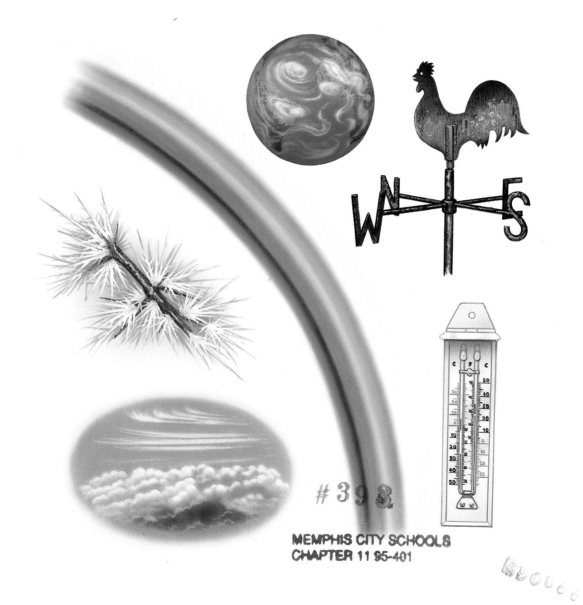

ANITA GANERI

Illustrated by Mike Atkinson and Mark Machin

FRANKLIN WATTS
NEW YORK•CHICAGO•LONDON•TORONTO•SYDNEY

© 1993 Franklin Watts

Franklin Watts, Inc.
95 Madison Avenue
New York, NY 10016

Library of Congress Cataloging–in–Publication Data

Ganeri, Anita, 1961–
    Weather / by Anita Ganeri.
        p.   cm. – (Nature detective)
    Includes index.
    Summary: Explains various aspects of weather including the whys
and wherefores of clouds, rain, hailstones, atmosphere, climate,
forecasting, and other related topics. Includes simple projects.
    ISBN 0–531–14250–7
    1. Weather – Juvenile literature.   2. Meteorology – Juvenile
literature   3. Weather – Experiments – Juvenile literature.
[1. Weather.   2. Meteorology.]   I. Title.   II. Series: Nature
detective (New York, N.Y.)
QC981.3.G37 1993
551.5 – dc20   92 – 26987
                                                            CIP AC

Editor: Sarah Ridley
Design: KAG Design Ltd

Consultants: Many thanks to Maurice Tall,
formerly of the Meteorological Office, Bracknell.

Printed in Belgium

Contents

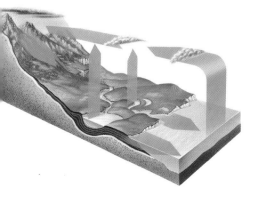

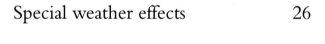

What is the weather?	4
Air and air pressure	6
Temperature and the sun	8
Moving water	10
What are clouds?	12
Why does it rain?	14
Snow and ice	16
What causes thunder and lightning?	18
How does the wind blow?	20
Different climates	24
Special weather effects	26
Weather forecasting	28
More things to do	30
Index	32

Woodland Presbyterian School

What is the weather?

What is the weather like today where you live? Is it overcast and cloudy, or sunny and warm, or even snowing? We often take the weather for granted, but it affects almost everything we do; from the type of clothes we wear, to the food we eat, to the type of buildings we live in. The weather is all around us, all the time. So there is always plenty for the weather detective to see.

Weather happens in the lowest layer of the atmosphere, the giant blanket of air that surrounds the earth. This layer is called the troposphere. It extends about 10 miles into the sky. The weather is the state of this air at any given time. The atmosphere, the sun, and water vapor are the main ingredients in the weather. The way they react together gives us our day to day weather, such as clouds, rain, fog, sunshine, and snow.

WARNING! WARNING! WARNING!
Never look directly into the sun as this can seriously damage your eyes.

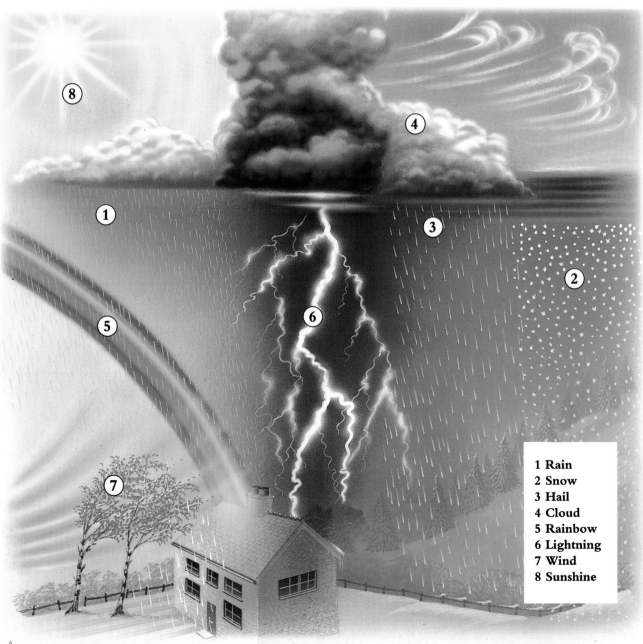

1 Rain
2 Snow
3 Hail
4 Cloud
5 Rainbow
6 Lightning
7 Wind
8 Sunshine

Why do we have weather?

The sun heats some parts of the earth more than others. The weather helps to spread this heat more evenly. Without weather, the tropics around the equator would get hotter and hotter. The Arctic and Antarctic would get colder and colder. Nothing would be able to live on earth.

Weather worship

Throughout history, people have worshiped various weather gods. The most important were the gods of the rain and the sun because these were vital for making crops grow. In Ancient Egypt, the pharaoh (king) was thought to be the son of the sun god. In Japan, the emperor was worshiped as a descendent of the sun goddess. In China, dragons were thought to bring rain which is so vital for growing crops such as rice. Some tribes still perform rain dances if there has been an unusually dry spell.

The Tower of the Winds in Athens, Greece, was built in the first century B.C. by the astronomer Andronicus. It has eight sides, each carved with a figure representing one of the eight main winds.

Weather watching

The scientific study of the weather is called meteorology. Professional meteorologists use a wide range of equipment to record and forecast the weather. You can make simple versions of some of these instruments for yourself. There are instructions for doing this throughout this book. To build up an accurate picture of the weather, you need to measure rainfall or snowfall, temperature, hours of sunshine, air pressure, wind speed and direction, and the amount of cloud covering the sky. If possible, take your measurements at a set time in the morning, at midday, and at a set time in the evening. See if your records match up with the forecast for the day. You can also tell a great deal about the weather simply by using your eyes. Here are some other items to help you.

Notebook Write down all your recordings in a notebook. Divide each page into columns, one for each aspect of the weather. Always make a note of the date, time, and any general comments about the weather conditions.
Colored pencils Quick sketches are a good way of recording the amount of cloud cover and the type of clouds, for example.
Magnifying glass This is useful for looking closely at snowflakes or frost.
Camera Cameras can be expensive and you don't need to buy one just for recording the weather. If you do have a camera already, though, you can take dramatic pictures of sunsets, sunrises, and other weather phenomena. Remember to write down the time and date on which you took a particular photograph.

Air and air pressure

Air is all around us and is what makes up the atmosphere. The atmosphere presses down on the earth creating what is called atmospheric pressure, or air pressure. This is measured in units called inches of mercury with instruments called barometers. Changes in air pressure bring changes in the weather. Rising air pressure usually brings sunny, settled weather. A fall in pressure will generally mean that cloudy, rainy weather is on its way.

The air presses down on you, too, but the fluids inside your body and your breathing balance out its effect so you cannot feel its weight.

The atmosphere

The atmosphere is divided into layers, each according to its height above the ground. The weather happens in the troposphere, the layer directly above the ground, where the air is constantly moving. This is the layer that we all live in. Here the air pressure is such that we can breathe easily.

Air pressure decreases the higher up you go. Aircraft fly in the layer above our troposphere, called the stratosphere. Due to the different air pressure and lack of oxygen high up, aircraft are designed with special pressurized cabins so that the passengers can breathe normally.

Air masses and fronts

An air mass is a huge expanse of air that can be hot, cold, wet, or dry. This depends on whether it formed over sea, land, in a warm area, or a cold one. Particular air masses are associated with certain parts of the world. As the air masses move above the earth, they affect the weather. There are four main types of air mass – tropical continental (hot and dry), tropical maritime (warm and moist), polar continental (cool and dry), and polar maritime (cool and moist).

When two air masses meet, they do not mix but form boundaries called fronts. Fronts often bring unsettled, stormy weather.

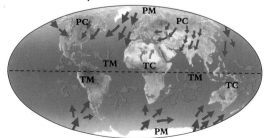

Tropical continental (TC) Polar continental (PC)
Tropical maritime (TM) Polar maritime (PM)

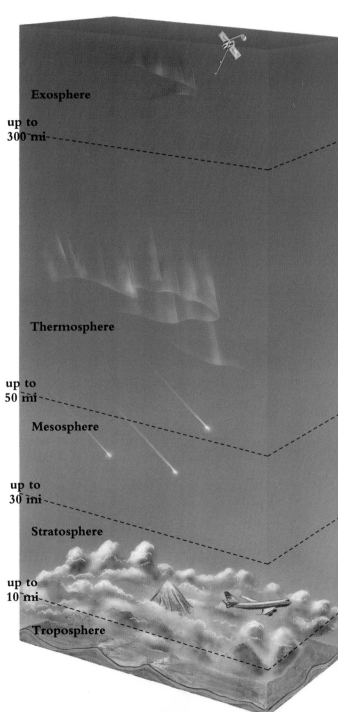

Exosphere

up to
300 mi

Thermosphere

up to
50 mi

Mesosphere

up to
30 mi

Stratosphere

up to
10 mi

Troposphere

Highs and lows

Air pressure varies in different parts of the world. Changes in air pressure are caused by air moving sideways into or out of columns of warmer or cooler air. In an area of low pressure, the air pressure is usually below 29.5 inches. Low pressure is associated with air rising, leading to cooling, clouds, and rain.

As air rises, it cools, gets heavier and starts to sink again. This creates an area of high pressure where the pressure is usually above 30.1 inches. High pressure is associated with air sinking, leading to dry, settled weather. In the summer, high pressure usually brings sunny, hot weather. In the winter, it can bring cold weather with frost or fog.

On a weather map, areas of equal pressure are linked by lines called isobars. On these maps, the closer together they are, the higher the wind speed. To find the nearest area of low pressure, stand with your back to the wind. It is on your left if you live in the Northern Hemisphere and on your right if you live in the Southern Hemisphere. The way that highs and lows move from day to day affects the kind of weather you get.

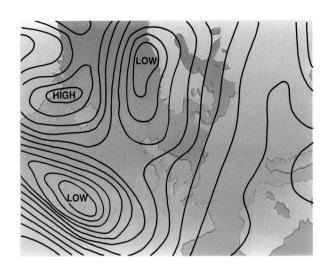

Aneroid barometer
This barometer is the most important weather instrument, recording changes in atmospheric pressure.

Make a barometer

To help you forecast the weather, record any rises and falls in air pressure using your own barometer.

You will need: a jelly jar; a balloon; a rubber band; glue; a drinking straw; some cardboard.

1. Warm the jelly jar in your hands for a few minutes. Then cut the neck off the balloon and stretch the rest tightly over the top of the jar. Hold it in place with the rubber band.

2. Cut one end of the straw to a point. Lay the straw across the surface of the stretched balloon and glue the unpointed end to the center of the "lid."

3. Mark a scale with high and low on the cardboard and attach a cardboard support to the back so the scale stands up.

4. Place your barometer next to the scale. As the air pressure rises or falls, the straw will move up or down the scale.

Temperature and the sun

The earth receives huge quantities of energy as heat and light from the sun. Without this energy, nothing could live on our planet. It would be much too cold. The earth receives just enough sunlight to keep its temperature between about -60°F and 130°F. It is a delicate balance. If the earth received just a tenth less sunlight, the oceans would ice over and everything would die.

The sun is the driving force behind the weather. Its heat stirs the atmosphere, causing the weather to happen. The sun's rays filter through the earth's atmosphere, warming the ground which, in turn, warms the air above it and makes it move. But the sun does not heat the earth equally and temperatures vary around the world. The areas around the equator are the hottest in the world. This is because the sun is high in the sky and its rays hit the earth directly, with full force. The poles are the coldest areas. Here the sun's rays strike at an angle because the earth's surface is curved. They spread over a larger area, and therefore their power is much reduced.

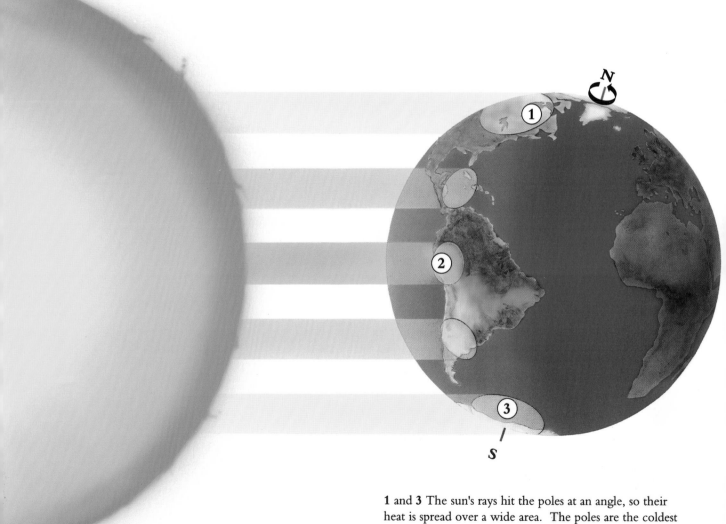

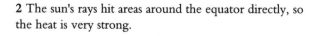

1 and **3** The sun's rays hit the poles at an angle, so their heat is spread over a wide area. The poles are the coldest places on the earth.

2 The sun's rays hit areas around the equator directly, so the heat is very strong.

Measuring sunshine and temperature

To record the amount of sunshine an area receives, meteorologists sometimes use an instrument called a sunshine recorder. One type consists of a glass ball that focuses the sunlight onto a strip of cardboard so it leaves a scorch mark. The length of the mark indicates the number of hours of sunshine in a day.

Thermometers are used to measure temperature in degrees Fahrenheit (°F), Centigrade, or Celsius (°C). They are usually kept in a boxlike shelter. This is placed outdoors and is raised about 5 feet above the ground to allow air to circulate around and through it.

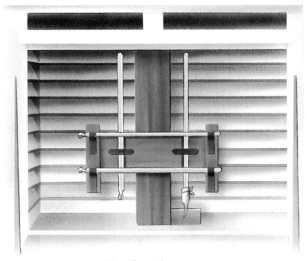

Weather thermometers

Sunshine recorder

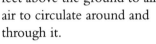

Taking the temperature

You can buy a thermometer from a hardware store or home center. Be very careful not to break your thermometer. It contains mercury which is poisonous.

Mount the thermometer on a piece of board and attach it to a north-facing wall or tree trunk. It should be in the shade and 5 feet above the ground. Take temperature readings three times a day - in the early morning, at midday, and in the early evening. See how they compare. The hottest time of the day is usually between midday and 3:00 pm. You should also write down what the weather is like at the time - you may be surprised with your results.

To convert degrees Fahrenheit into degrees Centigrade, subtract 32 from the degrees F, multiply the rest by 5, then divide the result by 9. To convert degrees Centigrade into degrees Fahrenheit, multiply the degrees C by 9, divide the result by 5, then add 32.

Moving water

Over two-thirds of the earth is covered in water. It lies in the oceans, lakes, and rivers, and is frozen in the ice caps. Water is also present in the atmosphere in its gas form, water vapor, and falls to earth as rain or snow. But any rain you see has already fallen billions of times before. This is because no new water is ever made on earth. The existing supply is recycled and reused time after time, in a continuous process called the water cycle.

In the water cycle, the sun heats the water in the oceans. It evaporates (turns into water vapor) and rises into the air. As it rises, it cools and condenses (turns into droplets of liquid water) into rain or condenses and then freezes into snow. This rain or snow falls back into the oceans or is carried by rivers to the sea. Billions of gallons of water evaporate from the oceans each day. The atmosphere contains enough water vapor to cover the earth with a layer 3 feet deep.

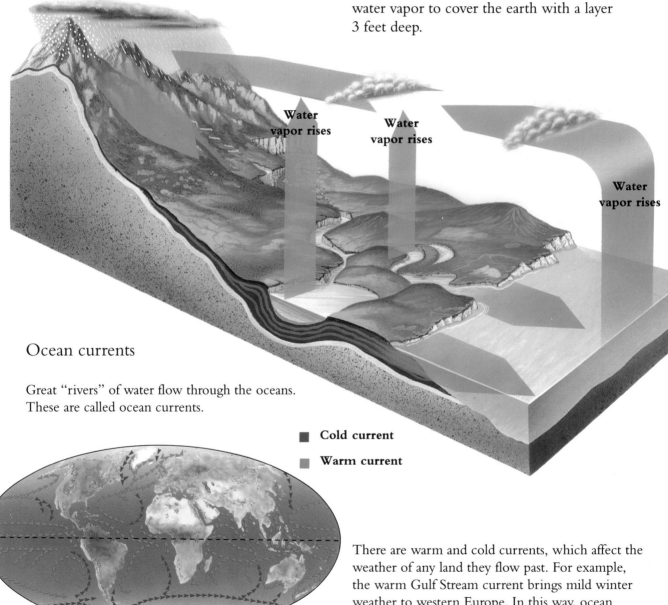

Water vapor rises

Water vapor rises

Water vapor rises

Ocean currents

Great "rivers" of water flow through the oceans. These are called ocean currents.

■ **Cold current**

■ **Warm current**

There are warm and cold currents, which affect the weather of any land they flow past. For example, the warm Gulf Stream current brings mild winter weather to western Europe. In this way, ocean currents help to spread the heat of the sun around the world.

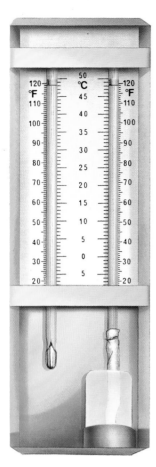

Wet and dry bulb hygrometer

Relative humidity

The amount of water vapor in the air is called humidity. Because warm air can hold more water vapor than cool air, there is often a lot of water vapor in the air on a hot summer's day.

Meteorologists measure "relative" humidity. This is the percentage of water vapor actually in the air compared to the maximum amount of water vapor the air could hold. It is measured with an instrument called a hygrometer.

In the past, human hair was used in hygrometers. Hair gets longer in moist air and shrinks in dry air. Today, a wet and dry bulb hygrometer is used instead. This is made up of two thermometers. One records the temperature of the air, as normal. The other has its bulb-end wrapped in wet muslin cloth. As water evaporates from the cloth, it cools the bulb. The drier the air, the cooler the bulb will become. Readings are taken from both thermometers. The greater the difference between the two, the lower the relative humidity. High humidity is linked with wet or foggy weather while low humidity is connected with dry weather.

Reaching the dew point

If you get up early and go outside, you may see drops of dew on the grass or on spiders' webs. Dew forms when the air cools at night and reaches a point where it cannot hold any more water vapor. This is called the dew point and the air is said to be "saturated." The water vapor then starts to condense into liquid form on leaves, grass, and objects. The dew soon evaporates again in the morning sun. The dew point is also the point at which clouds form, and with them, rain or snow (see pages 12-13).

A similar process happens when you breathe out on a cold day. You can see your breath as a white cloud because the water vapor in your breath has condensed into tiny water droplets.

Water watching

Try making your own miniature version of the water cycle to see how it works. Stand a small container, such as an egg cup, in a large bowl. Fill the bowl with water until it reaches about halfway up the egg cup. Cover the bowl with clear plastic wrap. Put a small weight, such as a pebble, on top.

Place the bowl in sunlight and watch what happens. The water in the bowl evaporates in the heat, rises and condenses as it comes into contact with the cooler plastic. Drops of water then fall back into the egg cup.

What are clouds?

Clouds form when the sun heats the ground and warm air rises and cools so that the water vapor it contains condenses into tiny droplets of water. This condensation often takes place around specks of dust or dirt, or particles of ice in the sky. A cloud is made up of millions upon millions of droplets.

Clouds are divided into two basic shapes, depending on how the warm air rises. Cumuliform, or "heap," clouds form when the sun heats patches of the ground and warm air rises rapidly in bubbles. These are common on hot, summer days. Stratiform, or "layer," clouds form when large masses of air rise slowly into the air. They are associated with overcast skies and rain.

Cumuliform clouds

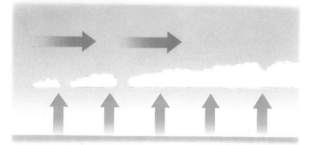

Stratiform clouds

The messages in the clouds

There are ten main types of clouds. They are classified according to their height above the ground, their shape, and the type of weather they bring. Once you have learned to identify the different clouds, you should soon be able to use them as clues to the weather.

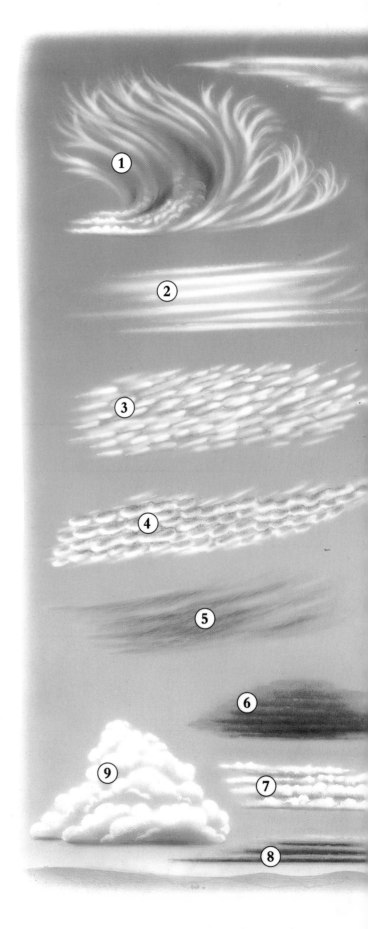

High level clouds (around 20,000 feet and up)

1 *Cirrus* These clouds look like wispy, curly streaks. They form so high up that they are made up of ice crystals. They usually signal bad weather.

2 *Cirrostratus* These are layers of milky-white cloud high in the sky. They are a sign of rain.

3 *Cirrocumulus* These form regular patterns of ripples in the sky. They warn of unsettled weather.

Middle level clouds (around 7,000–17,000 feet)

4 *Altocumulus* Flat gray and white blobs of cloud. They sometimes signal the onset of a thunderstorm after a sticky summer's day.

5 *Altostratus* Layers of dull, gray cloud which often warn that rain is on its way.

6 *Nimbostratus* "Nimbus" means rain in Latin. These thick, dark gray clouds bring rain or even snow.

Low level clouds (with their bases below 7,000 feet)

7 *Stratocumulus* These very common clouds look like gray or white rolls or round patches. They often signal dry weather.

8 *Stratus* Layers of dull, gray cloud which often bring rain, drizzle, or even snow.

9 *Cumulus* Fluffy white puffs of cloud which can appear on hot, sunny days.

10 *Cumulonimbus* Heavy dense clouds that form into towering shapes, the tops of which can reach as high as 40,000 feet. These clouds produce heavy showers or thunderstorms.

Fog, mist, and smog

Fog and mist are really just clouds that form on or near the ground. When visibility is over 0.6 miles, it is said to be misty. If it is less than this, it is foggy.

Smog is a mixture of smoke and fog, caused by water vapor condensing around pollution in the air. The worst smogs are the photochemical smogs that affect crowded cities. They are caused by sunlight reacting with fumes from car exhausts.

Why does it rain?

Look out for gloomy, dark gray clouds. They are a sure sign of rain. Raindrops form inside clouds in one of two ways. Sometimes hundreds of tiny water droplets inside a cloud collide with each other to form bigger drops. This process is called coalescence. When the drops are big and heavy enough, they fall as rain. Other raindrops form by condensation. Inside higher, colder clouds, water vapor freezes onto ice crystals. When they are heavy enough, they fall from the cloud as snow. They melt as they fall through warmer air, forming raindrops. Sleet is frozen rain. When water falls as rain or snow, it is called precipitation.

Coalescence   **Condensation**

Raindrops, drizzle, and showers

Raindrops look like flat-bottomed circles, not like teardrops as many people imagine. They are usually about 0.06 inch in diameter, although they can reach about 0.25 inch at most. When raindrops are less than 0.02 inch in diameter, it is drizzling.

Rainfall is described as light if less than 0.10 inch falls in an hour. It is heavy if more than 0.30 inch falls in an hour. Short bursts of rain with brighter periods in between are described as showers. Use the rain gauge (below) and these descriptions to help you record the rainfall where you live.

Drought and flood

Sometimes, an area receives much less rain than usual. The ground becomes very dry and dusty, and cracks may appear in the surface. This is what we call a drought. Plants and crops struggle to survive and water authorities may introduce rules to save water, such as a ban on using water hoses. Streams and small rivers will eventually dry up and the level in reservoirs and lakes will go down.

On the other hand, floods may occur when violent rainstorms or thunderstorms release so much rain onto the land that the water can't drain away fast enough. Floods can also appear when there has been a lot of rain over a period of time, so that the ground can no longer absorb the water. A sudden thaw of snow can also cause flooding.

AMAZING FACTS

Mount Waialeale in Hawaii has up to 350 days of rain a year.

The wettest place on earth is Tutunendo in Colombia. It has an average of 468 inches of rain a year.

The record rainfall for one day is 73.62 inches on the island of La Reunion in the Indian Ocean. The record for one month is held by Cherrapunji in India. In July 1861, the town had 366.14 inches of rain.

Measuring rainfall

Rainfall is measured in inches, using an instrument called a rain gauge. It records the amount of rain that would cover the ground if none of it evaporated or drained away. How much rain falls where you live? Make this simple rain gauge to find out. Take your readings at the same time every day and add them up to see how much rain has fallen over a week.

You will need: a jelly jar or a similar container; a funnel with the same diameter as the base of the jar; some masking tape; a waterproof marker; a ruler.

1. Cut a piece of masking tape and mark it every 0.1 inches. Stick the scale along the side of the jar.
2. Put the funnel into the neck of the jar and sink the jar into the ground. Make sure it is clear of overhanging trees or walls.
3. Make recordings at the same time every day of the level of rainfall. Calculate the rainfall for a week, then a month, then a whole year.

Snow and ice

Like raindrops, snowflakes form inside clouds. The clouds need to be high up enough to contain ice crystals. Water vapor condenses and freezes onto them until they are heavy enough to fall through the cloud. As they fall, they crash into other crystals to form flakes. If the air is cold enough, they fall as snow.

Snowflakes all have six sides but their shapes vary according to the temperature of the air. Rod- and needle-like shapes form in very cold air; star shapes in slightly warmer air. Whatever their shape, however, no two flakes are ever the same. Use your magnifying glass to look more closely at snowflakes. See how many different shapes you can find.

Measuring snowfall

The greatest snowfall over a year was 1,122 inches at Mount Rainier, in Washington. Your area hopefully gets much less, but you can measure any snowfall quite easily. You can simply stick a ruler into it to see how much is covering the ground. Find a place where the snow is even, not piled up in drifts.

Frosting over

Dew forms at night when the ground cools down and cools the air close to the ground so that it cannot hold its supply of water vapor any longer. If the temperature falls below freezing, the dew freezes and becomes frost. Look for delicate fern frost patterns on windowpanes and for spikes of hoar frost around keyholes, and on tree branches.

Freezing fog or drizzle can coat trees with a white dusting of ice. This is called rime.

Expanding ice

As water freezes, it expands. This is why the water pipes inside houses or apartments sometimes burst in winter.

To see this for yourself, fill a margarine tub with water. Put the lid on and put it in the freezer. After a few hours you will find that the lid has been forced off the tub by the ice.

How do hailstones form?

Hailstones are balls of ice, but they do not form when the weather is cold. They fall during thunderstorms which often happen on hot, sticky days. Hailstones form inside cumulonimbus storm

clouds. Violent air currents inside the cloud toss ice crystals up and down as many as twenty times. As they are bounced about, water freezes onto the crystals in layers, rather like the skins around an onion. When they are about the size and shape of peas, they fall to the ground as hail.

To see how many times a hailstone has been bounced up and down inside a cloud, quickly cut it in half and count the rings. Occasionally, some hailstones are bigger than golf balls!

17

What causes thunder and lightning?

A thunderstorm is one of the most spectacular types of weather. Look for the signs that a thunderstorm is forming on a warm, humid summer's day. First, huge gray cumulonimbus clouds start to form, darkening the sky. Then flashes of lightning light up the sky. Shortly afterward you can hear rumbles of thunder. Storms also bring gusty winds and pouring rain. So what causes all these special effects?

As a cumulonimbus cloud builds up, air currents inside the cloud cause a buildup of positive electrical charges (+) at the top, and negative charges (-) at the bottom. The ground is also positively charged. To equalize the charges, lightning flashes between positive and negative either inside the cloud (sheet lightning) or between the cloud and the ground (forked lightning).

The zigzag lightning you often see is actually the "return" stroke from the ground back to the cloud. It heats the air in its path to 55,000°F. This makes the air expand at high speed, causing the booming noise of thunder.

AMAZING FACTS

The only person to be struck by lightning seven times is Roy C. Sullivan, an American park ranger. On different occasions he lost his eyebrows, had his hair catch on fire twice, lost his big toenail, and suffered mild burns.

There are over 15 million thunderstorms a year, and about 6,000 flashes of lightning each second.

Lightning is caused by static electricity. This is the type of electricity you create when you comb your hair and it crackles.

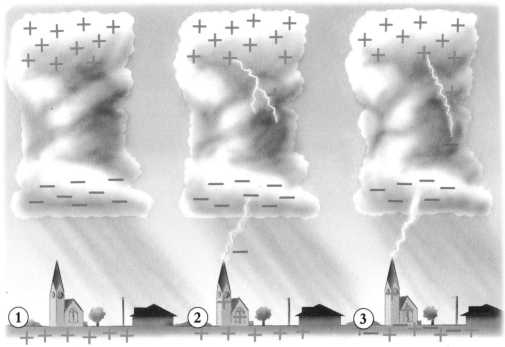

1 Electrical charges build up in the clouds; positive (+) at the top, negative (–) at the bottom.

2 Lightning flashes between the negative charges in the cloud and the positive charges on the ground.

3 Lightning flashes back from the ground, heating the air in its path. The air expands causing thunder.

Storm safety

Thunderstorms produce huge amounts of electricity, which can be dangerous if you are not careful. Lightning always takes the shortest route to the ground, putting tall trees and buildings at risk of being struck. A direct hit can completely demolish an old oak tree. You should **never** take shelter under a tree in a thunderstorm.

If you are caught in a storm, crouch down in the open. You are safe inside a car, because its rubber tires do not conduct (carry) electricity. Tall buildings, such as church steeples, are often protected by lightning conductors. These are strips of metal or cables that run down the side of the building to the ground. They carry the electricity down safely.

Finding a thunderstorm

Next time there is a thunderstorm near you, watch and listen carefully. Although the lightning and thunder happen at exactly the same time, you see the lightning before you hear the thunder. This is because light travels faster through the air than sound does. Lightning can reach a speed of up to 85,000 miles per second on its return journey. Sound travels through air at about only 1,100 feet per second.

You can use this to calculate how far away a storm is. Count the number of seconds between the lightning and the thunder. Then divide this by five to give you the distance in miles.

19

How does the wind blow?

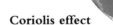

You cannot see the wind, but you can feel the effect it has on your face, see it blowing through the trees and whipping the sea into waves. Wind is moving air. It moves because of differences in both temperature and air pressure over the earth. Air moves from areas of high pressure (where cool, heavy air sinks) to areas of lower pressure (where warm, light air rises), creating wind. However, the winds do not blow directly from the poles to the equator, as you might think. As the earth spins on its axis, it drags the winds to the right in the Northern Hemisphere and to the left in the Southern Hemisphere. This is called the Coriolis effect.

You can see the pattern of the main world winds on the map, above. But what about the wind closer to home? Look at the weather records for your area to find out what the prevailing wind is. This is the most common type of wind an area has over a long period.

Different winds bring different weather conditions, depending on from which direction they blow. South winds are usually warm and fine; south westerlies are usually moist and

Trade winds The trade winds blow steadily toward the equator. Because of their reliability, sailors used to depend on them to guide their ships.

The doldrums The doldrums are the light, variable winds found in the ocean region around the equator. They are often accompanied by heavy rain, thunderstorms, and squalls.

warm; north winds are apt to be cold, and easterlies dry and the coldest of all in mid latitudes. Whichever way they blow, all the winds fulfill the same purpose, spreading the sun's heat more evenly around the world.

Winds in Northern Hemisphere

Winds in Southern Hemisphere

Coriolis effect

Measuring the wind

The two most important aspects of the wind to note are its direction and speed. Wind direction is measured with a weather vane, using the points of the compass as units. The wind direction is the direction the wind is blowing *from*. For example, a north wind is a wind blowing *from* the north.

Anemometers are used to measure wind speed. Spinning cup anemometers are the most common. The cups are attached to a vertical shaft. As they catch the wind, they spin and cause the shaft to spin too. The number of turns per minute is recorded and converted to miles per hour.

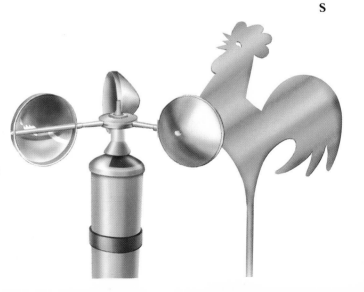

The Beaufort Scale

This international scale was devised in 1806 by Admiral Sir Francis Beaufort, to estimate wind speed at sea. It has since been adapted for use on land. By looking for clues about the effect of the wind, you can figure out roughly how fast the wind is blowing.

Beaufort Scale	Wind speed (mph)	Description	Effect on the land
Force 0	Under 1	Calm	Smoke rises vertically; trees are still.
Force 1	1–3	Light wind	Smoke drifts slowly with the wind.
Force 2	4–7	Light breeze	Leaves start to rustle.
Force 3	8–12	Gentle breeze	Leaves and twigs move; small flags out-stretched.
Force 4	13–18	Moderate wind	Small branches move; wind blows dust and paper about.
Force 5	19–24	Fresh wind	Wind makes small trees sway.
Force 6	25–31	Strong wind	Telephone wires whistle; too windy to use umbrellas; large branches move.
Force 7	32–38	Near gale	Whole trees begin to sway.
Force 8	39–46	Gale	Very difficult to walk against the wind; twigs snap off trees.
Force 9	47–54	Severe gale	Roof tiles and chimney pots are blown off.
Force 10	55–63	Storm	Wind uproots trees; structural damage to buildings.
Force 11	64–72	Severe storm	Severe and widespread damage.
Force 12	73	Hurricane	Severe destruction.

Make an anemometer

To make your own anemometer you will need: 4 plastic cups or yogurt cups (mark one of them with a large X); a sturdy piece of wood about 8 inches long to act as the shaft; 2 pieces of balsa wood, about 12 inches long; glue; a nail.

1. Glue the pieces of balsa wood together in a cross shape.

2. Glue the cups to the ends of the sticks. They must all face the same way.

3. Hammer the nail through the center of the cross into the wooden shaft.

4. Hold your anemometer up to the wind and see how fast it blows the cups around. Count how many times per minute the X-marked cup comes around.

21

Local winds around the world

There are many areas of the world that have a particular type of wind which affects the region's weather. Here are a few of them:

Buran (Russia and Central Asia) A strong, northeasterly wind. It often brings blizzards in winter.

Chinook (United States) A dry, warm westerly wind that blows in the Rocky Mountains. It is named after a local Indian tribe. It often signals the end of the winter's snow.

Föhn (Europe) A dry, warm wind that blows down the sides of the Alps. It is said to be the cause of headaches, depression, and even suicides.

Haboob (Sudan) The name given to dust storms of the Sudan area. They occur from about May to September, most often in the afternoon or evening.

Harmattan (Northwest Africa) A cool, dry northeasterly (or sometimes easterly) wind that carries dust with it.

Levanter (Mediterranean) An easterly wind that is most common in summer. It brings mild weather.

Mistral (Southern France) A very strong northwesterly wind that is dry and cold.

Pampero (Argentina) A very cold southwesterly wind. It blows from the Andes across the plains, often bringing storms.

Sirocco (North Africa) A southerly wind that blows from the Sahara Desert. It is hot, dry and can be very dusty.

Land and sea breezes

If you live or spend vacations near the coast, you may notice that the wind changes. During the day, sea breezes flow inland. At night, they flow out to sea. This is because, on a sunny day, the land heats up more quickly than the sea. Warm air rises over the land and cool air rushes in from the sea to replace it. At night, the pattern is reversed. The land cools down more quickly than the sea, so warm air rises over the sea and cool air rushes out from the land to replace it.

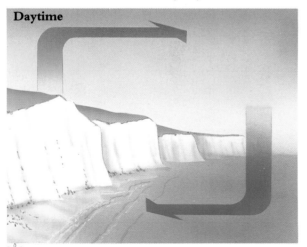

Daytime

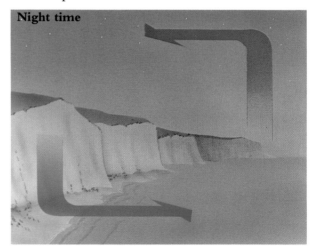

Night time

What are hurricanes?

You may never experience a hurricane where you live, but you may well hear or read about them in the news. Hurricanes are enormous tropical storms that look like gigantic spinning wheels of cloud. They begin over warm oceans. Warm air rises and cumulonimbus clouds start to form. As more air is added, the storm starts to spin and grow.
A hurricane can be 500 miles wide, with winds blowing at up to 225 mph. It generally moves westward, bringing torrential rain, howling winds, and causing huge waves which can devastate islands in its path. Hurricanes die down as they pass over land, and blow themselves out. At the center of the storm is a clear, calm area, called the "eye." There is a short lull in the storm as the eye passes overhead.

Hurricanes are also known as typhoons in the Pacific, cyclones in the Indian Ocean, and willy willies in Australia. Individual hurricanes are given names from an alphabetical list drawn up each year. They were first named by an Australian meteorologist, Clement Wragge, in the nineteenth century. He named them after people he disliked! Some famous hurricanes include Celeste and Hugo.

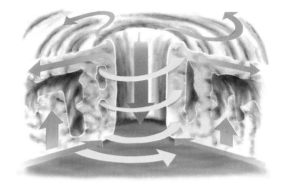

What are tornadoes?

Tornadoes are much smaller storms than hurricanes, but even more violent. They are also called twisters or whirlwinds because they consist of spinning funnels of wind that hang down from thunderclouds. The winds twist as hot air is sucked up. Inside the funnel, winds can blow at over 280 mph. As a tornado "leapfrogs" across land, it sucks up anything in its path, including people, cars, and trains. It can uproot trees, tear the roofs from buildings, and blow out windows.

Tornadoes are common in summer in the midwestern United States. "Tornado Alley" stretches from Texas to Illinois.

Different climates

What is the difference between weather and climate? Weather is the state of the air from day to day, whereas climate is the average pattern of weather a place has over a very long period of time. The climate of a place depends on several things – its latitude, its closeness to the sea, its physical features, such as mountains, and its prevailing winds and ocean currents. What type of climate do you live in? Would you prefer to live somewhere else? You can see where the main climate bands lie on the map below.

The earth's major climates

Polar The regions around the North and South poles are cold and windy all year around. Temperatures can fall below -60°F and there are frequent blizzards. Winter is long and dark, whereas the sun never sets in summer.

Tropical Around the equator, the climate is hot, wet, and humid most of the year.

Temperate Mild winters and warm summers make this the most balanced type of climate, and the most pleasant. Only seven percent of the earth has a temperate climate, yet it is home to nearly half of the earth's population.

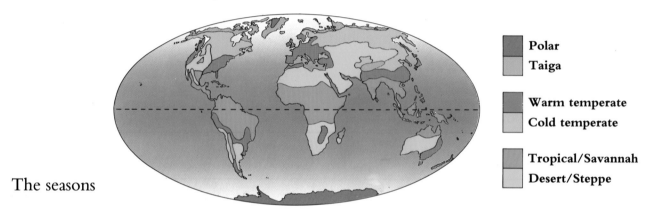

- Polar
- Taiga
- Warm temperate
- Cold temperate
- Tropical/Savannah
- Desert/Steppe

The seasons

In places with a temperate climate, there are four seasons a year. They are caused by the earth tilting on its axis as it orbits the sun. One hemisphere leans toward the sun and has summer, while the other has winter. Then the positions are reversed. In between, it is spring or fall.

The equator is never tilted away from the sun, so the tropics do not have seasons. Instead, they are either hot and wet, or hot and dry all the year around. At the poles, it is either dark and freezing cold in the winter, or light and freezing cold in the summer!

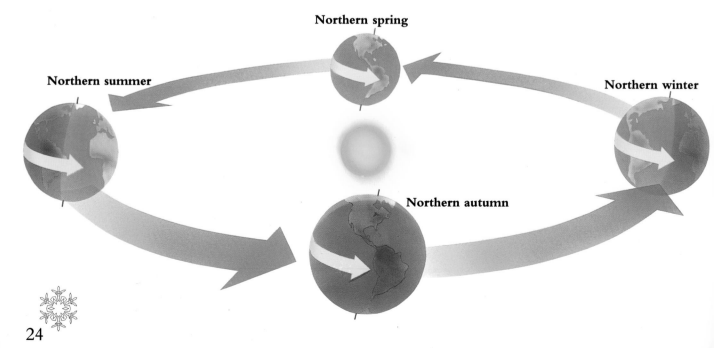

Northern spring

Northern summer

Northern winter

Northern autumn

Heat and color

You can test it with two thermometers and a piece of black cloth or paper and a piece of white cloth or paper. Put the bulb end of each thermometer under the two different pieces of cloth and leave them in the sun. Read the temperatures every 10 minutes to see which is the quickest to warm up. It should be the thermometer under the black cloth.

The poles are the coldest places on earth. This is partly because the sun's rays hit them at an angle and partly because they are covered in white ice and snow. Light colors tend to reflect heat away, whereas dark colors absorb heat. This is called the albedo effect.

Why does the climate change?

The earth's climate changes naturally over millions of years. At the moment we are in a warm period, called an interglacial. The last glacial, or Ice Age, ended about 10,000 years ago. A third of the earth lay under ice hundreds of feet thick.
Climatologists believe that these changes are caused by slight "wobbles" in the earth's path around the sun. The next Ice Age may begin in about 1,000 years' time.

Climatologists are more worried about the effect that people are having on the climate. By burning fossil fuels (oil and coal) and rain forest trees we are sending huge amounts of gases, such as carbon dioxide, high into the atmosphere. (By cutting down the trees, there is also more carbon dioxide present in the air as living trees absorb this gas through photosynthesis.) This is stopping excess heat escaping from the earth. If this continues, the earth's temperature could rise by up to 7°F by the year 2030. Some scientists think it could rise even higher. This could melt the ice at the poles, raising sea levels by up to 200 feet and flooding low-lying coastal cities, such as London, New York, and Sydney.

Another cause for concern is the thinning of the ozone layer high above the earth. Ozone is a form of oxygen. It acts like a sunscreen, shielding us from the sun's harmful ultraviolet (UV) rays which can cause skin cancer and stop plants from growing. In 1985, scientists discovered a hole in the ozone layer above Antarctica. Again, people are to blame. The ozone is being destroyed by man-made gases, called CFCs (chlorofluorocarbons). They are found in aerosol sprays, refrigerators, and styrofoam packaging. Always look for "ozone friendly" products when you go shopping.

Special weather effects

Sometimes the weather produces dramatic and spectacular special effects. In the past, many of these were thought to be signs from weather gods and spirits. On these two pages, however, you can find out how they happen, scientifically.

The colors of the rainbow

Watch for rainbows when the sun comes out after a shower of rain. To see the rainbow, stand with your back to the sun, facing the shower.

Sunlight is normally invisible. It is called white light, but it is made up of a mixture of colors. These colors are red, orange, yellow, green, blue, indigo, and violet - the colors of the spectrum. Raindrops act like tiny prisms. They bend the sunlight and split it into its different colors. In a rainbow, red is always at the top. Sometimes, double bows form. The second bow is fainter and the order of the colors is reversed.

From the ground you see a rainbow as a semicircle. From aircraft, they appear as full circles. The best times to see rainbows are in the morning or early evening, when the sun is low in the sky.

Sunrise and sunset

A clear, cloudless sky looks blue because particles of gas and dust in the air split sunlight into its various colors. Blue has the shortest wavelength and is bent most by the gas and dust. This means it is scattered all over the sky and toward our eyes.

At dawn and dusk, the sky turns a brilliant orange-red color as the sun rises or sets. This is because the sun's rays now have to travel farther through the atmosphere to reach our eyes. Red has the longest wavelength and is the only color that gets through.

Seeing things

Have you ever walked along the street on a very hot day and seen what you thought was a puddle of water ahead? This is an optical illusion, called a mirage. The puddle disappears as you get closer to it. Mirages are caused by light shining through layers of air of different temperatures. A layer of cold, heavy air lies over a layer of warm, light air. These layers reflect the light of the sky and distort it. Your brain is tricked into thinking that the distorted reflection looks like water. This is what happens to thirsty travelers in the desert when they think they see a welcome oasis of water in the distance.

Halos around the sun

Misty white halos sometimes appear around the sun, and even around the moon. These are caused by

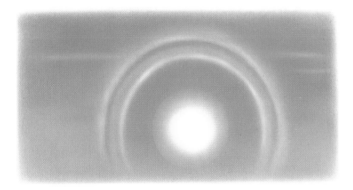

layers of cirrostratus clouds high up in the sky. Ice crystals in the clouds bend the sunlight so that it forms a circular halo. For hundreds of years these halos have been interpreted, quite correctly, as signs of rain or bad weather.

Fish and frog showers

In August 1921, frogs rained down on London! There have been many other reports of animals falling from the sky, including frogs, fish, crabs, tadpoles, and even flocks of geese. The most likely explanation for this seems to be that the animals were sucked out of ponds by strong whirlwinds or tornadoes, carried through the air, and dropped some distance away.

Make your own rainbows

You can make a rainbow outside using a garden hose. Wait until the sun is quite low in the sky in the early evening. Stand with your back to the sun and turn on the hose. When you look into the spray, you should see the colors of the rainbow as the drops of water split the sunlight.

To make a rainbow indoors, you will need a straight-sided glass of water and a piece of white paper. Put the paper on a sunny windowsill and stand the glass on it. Close the curtains until just a slit of light shines through onto the glass. The light will go through the water, split into its various colors, and appear as the spectrum on the paper.

Weather forecasting

All kinds of people rely on weather forecasts. For farmers, sailors, and pilots bad weather can mean ruined harvests or dangerous journeys. Even if you are just going for a walk or on a picnic, it is useful to know what the weather will be like so that you can wear the right clothes ... or stay at home!

In the past, people used natural signs to help them. By watching the behavior of certain animals and plants, they would predict the type of weather that lay ahead. Today, meteorologists are highly trained and have sophisticated equipment to help them make their predictions. They are skillful weather detectives, collecting clues and analyzing the results. The information is plotted on a chart, and fed into a computer to make forecasts.

Collecting information

A whole network of weather stations and meteorologists are needed to produce the weather maps you see on television or in the newspaper. There are about 10,000 weather stations around the world – on land and on ships out at sea. Every few hours, they take measurements of air pressure, cloud cover, temperature and hours of sunshine, wind speed and direction, humidity, and rain or snowfall. All this information is translated into an international code and sent to meteorological offices all over the world.

Radiosonde Balloons carry weather instruments 120,000 feet up into the atmosphere. Information about air pressure, humidity, and temperature is radioed back to the ground continuously. The radiosonde also carries a radar reflector which sends back information to the ground, enabling specialists to calculate the wind speed and direction.

Satellites Cameras on board weather satellites send back photographs of snow cover, cloud cover, temperature patterns, and the progress of storms.

Weather buoys These drift in the sea and transmit information about ocean currents and sea conditions back to land. The temperature of the sea at various depths is also recorded.

Radar Radar is used to track storms and to locate rain. Rain and snow show up as white on the screen.

Natural forecasting

People used to think that if cows lay down in their field, rain was on the way. But this doesn't seem to be true very often. A more accurate guide is the scarlet pimpernel. Its flowers shut tight when rain is in the air and open wide when the weather is sunny and dry.

February 2 is called Groundhog Day. Tradition says that if the groundhog sees its shadow on February 2, there will be six more weeks of cold weather. This has not proved a very reliable forecast.

Preparing a forecast

By taking the average of the readings you and your schoolfriends have been taking every day, you should be able to draw up your own weather chart for your area. Draw a map of where you live, or trace one from an atlas. Then plot the various types of weather you have observed. You can use the symbols shown above or make up your own weather shorthand. This can be useful for making quick records. Try making daily maps for a week or a month. It might be interesting to compare them with those drawn up by professionals.

Weather maps

The information gathered is then plotted on a special map, called a synoptic chart. The details are also fed into huge supercomputers to produce a forecast. The largest computers are in the weather centers at Bracknell, Great Britain, and Washington. They can do millions of calculations a second. The meteorologists also prepare the maps that will appear on television and in the newspapers. The computer's predictions are then checked and adjusted by human forecasters. It is possible to produce an accurate forecast for about a week ahead. The symbols used for these vary slightly from place to place, but you should be able to recognize them quite easily.

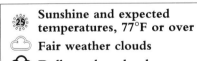

- ☀ **Sunshine and expected temperatures, 77°F or over**
- ☁ **Fair weather clouds**
- ☁ **Dull weather clouds**
- ☁ **Sunny intervals**
- ☁ **Rain**
- ☁ **Showers and sunny intervals**
- ☁ **Snow**
- ☁ **Hail**
- ☁ **Sleet**
- ☁ **Thunderstorms**
- ㉑ **Degrees above 32°F**
- ④ **Degrees below 32°F**

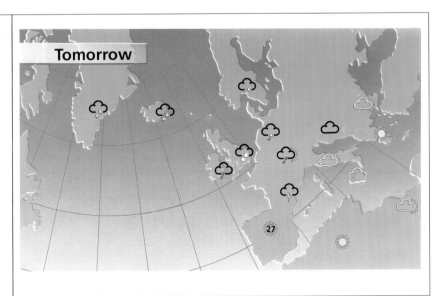

Tomorrow

More things to do

Keeping a weather scrapbook

You can record any unusual or interesting weather in a scrapbook. This will make a useful companion to your logbook. If the weather is particularly hot or cold, if there is a freak hailstorm or fall of snow, cut out any articles or pictures that appear in the newspaper. Stick them in your scrapbook, together with the weather map published for that day. Don't forget to write the date at the top of the page.

You can also record your own observations, through photographs or sketches. Chart the changing cloud formations over a whole day, taking a photograph or making a sketch every two hours from dawn to dusk.

Messages from nature

Instead of using meteorological instruments, try some traditional ways of forecasting the weather. If you live near the sea, find a piece of seaweed such as kelp. Hang it outdoors. It should shrivel and dry up in fine, warm weather but become moist and swollen if the air is moist and rain is on the way.

A pinecone is another natural forecaster, and a fairly reliable one, too. A pinecone opens its scales in warm, dry weather to let its seeds out. But it closes its scales tightly if rain is approaching. Again, your pinecone needs to be outside to help you forecast the weather.

Measuring the amount of water in snow

To see how much water a lump of snow contains, collect some snow in a jar. Don't press it down or

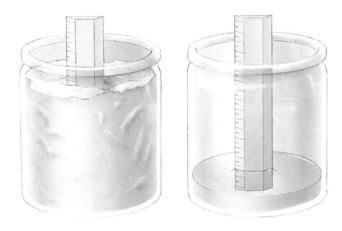

squash it. Measure how many inches of snow you have collected. Then take the snow inside and let it melt. Measure the depth of the water it leaves behind. You should get about one inch of water for every 10 inches of snow.

Calculating cloud cover

To measure how much of the sky is covered in clouds, meteorologists divide the sky into tenths. Zero tenths means that the sky is clear. Ten tenths means that it is completely overcast. Is it cloudy today where you live? Try to estimate how much of the sky is covered.

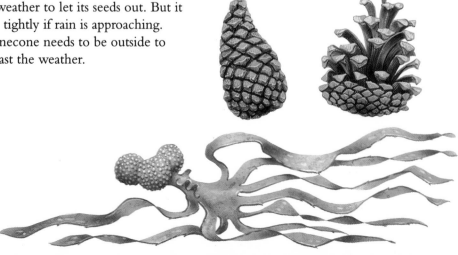

Making a weather vane

You can make your own weather vane for measuring wind direction. Ask an adult to cut the wood for you.

You will need: 3 balsa wood triangles (sizes are given below); balsa glue; 2 large beads; a long nail; a piece of dowel rod or a broom handle; a compass.

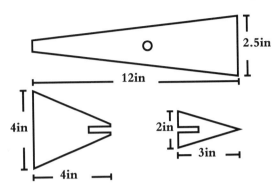

1. Use the compass to mark the points of the compass on the sides of the dowel rod. Push it into the ground so that the points are facing in the right directions.

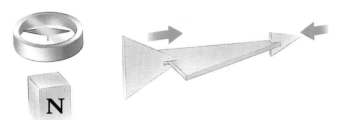

2. Glue the two smaller triangles in position on the front and back of the larger triangle.
3. Find the center of the vane, mark it, and thread the vane and the beads onto the nail.

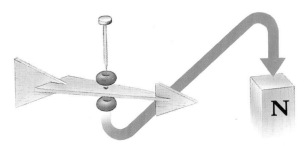

4. Hammer the vane into the top of the dowel rod. The pointer will show which direction the wind is blowing from.

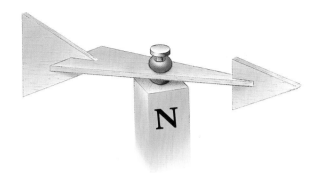

Making a wind speed gauge

To make a simple gauge to measure wind speed, you will need: a protractor; a Ping Pong ball; a length of strong thread.

1. Tape one end of the thread to the Ping Pong ball and tie the other end around the center of the protractor.

2. Take the gauge outside. Hold it level and parallel to the wind.
3. When the wind blows the ball, read the angle of the thread on the protractor. Figure out the wind speed from the scale [below].

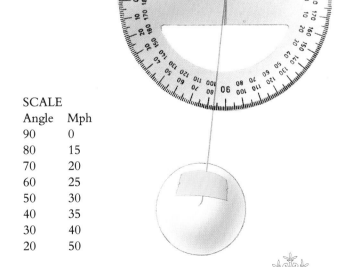

SCALE

Angle	Mph
90	0
80	15
70	20
60	25
50	30
40	35
30	40
20	50

Index

air masses 6
air pressure 6, 7, 20
albedo effect 25
altocumulus clouds 13
altostratus clouds 13, 27
anemometers 20, 21
aneroid barometers 7
atmosphere 4, 6, 8, 10, 25

barometers 6, 7
Beaufort Scale 21
blue skies 26
breezes, land and sea 22
Buran 22

Campbell-Stokes sunshine recorder 9
CFCs (chlorofluorocarbons) 25
Chinook 22
cirrocumulus clouds 13
cirrostratus clouds 13, 27
cirrus clouds 13
climates 24-5
cloud cover 30
clouds 11, 12-13, 14
coalescence 14
condensation 10, 11, 12, 14
Coriolis effect 20
cumuliform clouds 12
cumulonimbus clouds 13, 17, 18, 23
cumulus clouds 13
cyclones 23

dew 11, 17
dew point 11
doldrums 20
drizzle 14, 17
drought 15

equator 8, 24
evaporation 10, 11
exosphere 6

fish and frog showers 27
floods 15
fog 13
Föhn 22
freezing fog 17
fronts 6
frost 17

glacials 25
global warming 25
Gulf Stream 10

Haboob 22
hailstones 17
halos 27
Harmattan 22
humidity 11
hurricanes 22, 23
hygrometers 11

ice 17
Ice Ages 25
interglacials 25
isobars 7

Levanter 22
lightning 18, 19

mesosphere 6
meteorology 5, 28-9
mirages 27
mist 13
Mistral 22
mythology 5

natural forecasting 28, 29, 30
nimbostratus clouds 13

ocean currents 10
ozone layer 25

Pampero 22
photochemical smogs 13
polar climate 24
poles 8, 24, 25
pollution 13
precipitation 14

radiosonde 28
rain dances 5
rain gauges 14, 15
rainbows 26, 27
raindrops 14
rainfall 10, 14-15
rime 17

seasons 24
showers 14
Sirocco 22

sleet 14
smog 13
snow 10, 14, 16, 30
snowflakes 16
stratiform clouds 12
stratocumulus clouds 13
stratosphere 6
stratus clouds 13
sun 8
sunlight 8, 9, 26
sunrise and sunset 26
synoptic charts 29

temperate climate 24
temperatures 8, 9
thaws 15
thermometers 9, 11
thermosphere 6
thunderstorms 18-19
tornadoes 23, 27
Torro Intensity Scale 23
Tower of the Winds 5
trade winds 20
tropical climate 24
troposphere 4, 6
twisters 23
typhoons 23

water cycle 10, 11
water vapor 10, 11, 12, 16, 17
weather buoys 28
weather forecasts 28-9
weather gods 5
weather maps 7, 29
weather satellites 28
weather stations 28, 29
weather vanes 20, 31
whirlwinds 23, 27
willy willies 23
wind chill 22
wind direction 20, 31
wind speeds 20, 21, 22, 31
winds 20-2

PRINTED IN BELGIUM BY

INTERNATIONAL BOOK PRODUCTION